TERROR CRUISE

BARTLETT BROTHERS
TERROR CRUISE
ROGER ELWOOD

WORD
Kids!

WORD PUBLISHING
Dallas · London · Vancouver · Melbourne

TERROR CRUISE

Scripture quotations are from *International Children's Bible, New Century Version,* copyright © 1983, 1986, 1988 by Word Publishing, Dallas, Texas 75039.

Library of Congress Cataloging-in-Publication Data

Elwood, Roger.
    Terror cruise / Roger Elwood.
      p. cm.—(The Bartlett brothers)
    "Word Kids!"
    Summary: Teenage brothers Ryan and Chad and their father, a special envoy for the State Department, embark on a Caribbean cruise that becomes a journey into terror.
    ISBN 0–8499–3302–1
    [1. Caribbean Area—Fiction. 2. Brothers—Fiction.
3. Mystery and detective stories.] I. Title. II. Series:
Elwood, Roger. Bartlett brothers.
PZ7. E554Te 1991
[Fic]—dc20   91–13848
                                              CIP
                                                  AC

Printed in the United States of America

1 2 3 4 5 6 9 RRD 9 8 7 6 5 4 3 2 1

To KATE
—who will be reading
this series someday

One

Andrew Bartlett could drown at any time. He was pinned face down under a piece of metal that had been torn loose from the bulkhead in his room on the S.S. *Oceanic*. There had been a sudden and very powerful explosion elsewhere on the cruise ship on which he and his sons Ryan and Chad were supposed to be taking a vacation.

For several minutes, Mr. Bartlett drifted in and out of consciousness as the water level rose higher and higher.

"Oh, Dad!" fourteen-year-old Ryan Bartlett said, as he stood beside his father. He was trying somehow to lift the twisted, heavy chunk of metal off his dad's back. But he couldn't. It would have been a challenge even for his brother Chad, who was two years older and far stronger than Ryan probably ever would be.

"No more!" Mr. Bartlett told him. "It won't work. Go up on the main deck, Ryan. Please, see if you can get help there!"

The ship moved a little, the salt water rising a fraction of an inch higher as a result.

"I—I can't leave you," Ryan replied, his voice not much below an hysterical scream.

"You *have* to," Mr. Bartlett insisted. "It does no good just staying here. You can't lift it alone, son. That's nothing to be ashamed of. Besides, Chad may need your help. Go, Ryan, go *now!*"

"Chad can *always* take care of himself."

Andrew Bartlett turned his head slightly.

"Don't ever assume that. *I* can usually do the same, can't I? I've been held at gunshot, had grenades explode only a few feet away, been stabbed and beaten, and come through everything without lasting injury. But look at me now, Ryan. This is far different."

He raised his voice.

"Ryan. Listen to me. Like I told you before, get help outside. And . . . and, son, try to find Chad. *Do it!*"

Ryan leaned over and kissed his father on the forehead.

"What if I come back, what if *we* come back and . . . and you're —."

"We're all in the Lord's hands, no matter what happens. Don't *ever* forget that, don't ever."

Ryan turned reluctantly away from his father and waded through the water that had risen to just below his knees. When he reached the doorway, he paused for barely a second and looked back.

Andrew Bartlett was in a first class passenger's compartment on a large ocean liner that had been sabotaged by an explosion of unknown origin. Part of a metal wall had caved in on him, driving him nearly to the floor before part of the bunk bed slid under him. Now he was trapped face down on the bed with heavy metal on his back. He was in no immediate danger from the rising water level, but as the ship continued to sink, he would be.

"Good-bye, Dad," Ryan said. "I'll be back soon."

His father managed an expression that could only mean *hurry.*

Ryan ran outside. There was panic on the main deck. People were screaming and running, frantically searching for family and friends.Crew members were trying to keep the passengers from any action that was harmful.

Lord, where's my brother? he prayed to himself. *Show me what to do, where to go.*

The *S. S. Oceanic* had abruptly begun to tilt toward its left side.

Walking or running along the deck required skill. Ryan knew that Chad, with his well-trained athletic body, was better equipped for this kind of thing than he ever would be. The only part of him that got anything like regular exercise was his fingers when he was using his highly advanced computer at home.

3

Suddenly the ship seemed to groan, like a very large animal that was dying. Ryan was knocked off his feet, along with a great many other passengers.

"Dad!" he cried, looking over his shoulder, toward where he had just left his father. "I've got—."

He turned to go back, then remembered that at least he knew where his father was.

Not so with Chad.

The ship was several city blocks long, with three levels below the promenade/main deck. Finding his brother would be another part of the continuing nightmare that had begun.

Ryan managed to get to his feet.

Where was Chad when I saw him the last time? Where—?

In the gameroom!

Yes! He was showing that girl how to play billiards.

Ryan tried to remember how to get to the gameroom, but he couldn't. He was getting a sick feeling in his stomach, along with a heavy dose of guilt.

How can I? he told himself. *The cruise only started two days ago. I don't know where the—?*

A large man in his mid forties rushed up beside him. Startled, Ryan jumped to one side.

"Sorry," the man said, blushing.

Ryan studied his face for a second or two. The man was obviously nervous and upset.

"I saw you and your brother with Becky, my daughter, didn't I?" he asked. "I mean, I—."

4

Ryan's eyes widened. "Do you know where the gameroom is, sir?" he asked.

"Yes, I do. Do you think that's where they might be, son?"

"Yeah. I . . . I pray that—."

"Pray? Are you a—?"

Ryan nodded.

"Praise God! " the man said. Then he introduced himself, "I'm Raymond Houck."

"Ryan . . . Ryan Bartlett."

"Come with me, Ryan. The gameroom is on the next level."

They carefully made their way along the deck of the huge ocean liner, not knowing when the stricken ship would lurch again and throw them off balance.

The next movement wasn't long in coming. This time it proved to be quite a bit more violent. Ryan and Mr. Houck had to hold onto a nearby metal railing after losing their balance.

Out of the corner of his eye, Ryan could see that an elderly couple was not so fortunate. They tumbled overboard, their screams tearing through the air only briefly. Mr. Houck and Ryan were near a pile of life preservers. They each grabbed one and raced to the edge of the ship, throwing the preservers over the side. The couple grabbed these and hung on. There was nothing else Ryan and Mr. Houck could do, except pray that rescuers would come soon.

The stairway leading to the next level had buckled under the force of the blast and would not take much weight.

"I'm too big, Ryan," Mr. Houck told him. "It'll never support me. But I think you can make it. You've *got* to do it, Ryan. I'll tell you how to get to the gameroom. It's not far. I'll wait here as long as possible."

Alone! Ryan had to go the rest of the way alone.

The stairway had been pulled loose from the main deck level, but it was still attached to the floor just below. Mr. Houck lowered Ryan cautiously onto the top step, pausing to see if the metal stairs would move at all.

They did, too much so.

"It doesn't feel very solid, Ryan," Mr. Houck said, his voice hoarse and trembling. "It . . . it . . . might collapse . . . underneath you. There's got . . . to be another—."

"No!" Ryan shouted. "Nobody knows when the ship will sink some more. It's gotta be now! They could be goners. Time's—."

As though in reply to what he had just said, the giant ship groaned yet again.

The stairway started to move further away from the deck. Mr. Houck was caught off balance, and fell back.

Ryan was torn from his grasp !

Two

The gameroom was located directly below the promenade deck. It was just two doors down the corridor from the ship's library and reading room.

After a few minutes of talking to Becky Houck about school and movies, Chad Bartlett decided to show his terrific-looking new friend how to play billiards.

"It's a great game," he said. "Would you like to try?"

She nodded, her red hair glistening under the bright overhead lights in the gameroom.

"You'll enjoy it!"

They stood and walked over to the deluxe table, with its hand-carved legs and heavy Italian slate top covered by expensive English felt.

"Now, this is the cue," he said, as he took two off the dark wood rack and handed her one.

"Hey, there, funny guy, I know *that* much!" she protested. Becky wiggled her nose in a way that made Chad very glad he had bumped into her on the promenade deck.

He had gotten to the point where he was trying to show her how to hold the long narrow billiard cue. Just then, a bomb planted two levels down in the engine room of the *S. S. Oceanic* went off, sending shock waves throughout the entire ship.

Chad had put his arm around Becky's waist and positioned her fingers on the cue when—.

The two of them were knocked off their feet. Chad fell to one side, unable to hold on to Becky.

He caught a glimpse of her being hit a glancing blow by one of the round rubberized corners of the billiard table. She was then knocked like a helpless rag doll in the opposite direction from which he had been sent tumbling. An instant later the heavy billiard table slammed against the wall between them, buckling it outward.

The ceiling of that room had been tiled in mirrored glass with gold-colored specks in it. These square sections were supposedly anchored by heavy black glue as well as a metal frame around each piece.

Not enough glue, not nearly enough.

Scores of tiles were jarred away from the ceiling, some tumbling immediately, others seconds later. But the rest were hanging loosely, dropping one by one by—.

"Becky!" Chad screamed, shaking his head, trying to clear it so that he could get to his feet and stay there. He started to stand. But he fell back a split second before a chunk of jagged glass hit the floor where he had just been. It landed so close, in fact, that the sharp edge sliced into one of the new tennis shoes he was wearing.

The lights blinked but didn't go out. Chad propped himself up on his elbows, looking for Becky.

There she was! In the opposite corner at the other end of the room . . . her head hanging limply to one side.

Oh, Lord, oh, Lord, help me, Chad whispered. *Help me to get to her, and . . . help Dad and Ryan wherever they are.*

The ship shook again! That sound . . . steel supports shuddering under the structural strain generated by the bomb blast!

Chad could feel the floor tilt a bit more. He spread his hands out to either side of him, careful not to touch any of the fallen glass nearby.

Groaning!

He could hear Becky groaning!

I have to get to her. She needs—.

Chad tried once more to stand and succeeded.

Chad knew that he would probably have some bruises. But, otherwise, he didn't seem to be injured.

9

He started cautiously across the room, aware that the enormous ship might lurch again and—.

It seemed that, for every few inches he managed to move forward, another piece of glass plunged down. Thankfully, most of these were not anywhere near him, except for the very large one that hit his shoulder just before he reached Becky's sprawled form.

Chad cried out and almost fell as pain hit him. The ship was steady for the moment, so he was able to continue standing with a little less effort. He tried to concentrate on getting the glass out, hoping that it wouldn't shatter further until he had pulled it free.

In a flash he remembered the wrestling injury he'd received a year or so earlier. His leg had been nearly broken at the knee, and the pain had hit him like a heavy-weight boxer's knockout punch.

In that single, awful moment of pain, Chad had had to will himself not to pass out. If he had fallen on his leg, the injury would have been worse. His high school's wrestling team was there, so was their coach. But it would have taken a second or two for anyone to reach him, and he didn't have that much time.

I will not weaken, he had told himself. *I will fall back, away from my leg, and not forward or to the side. I will do this because, yes, Lord, You have made me strong enough to do it!*

And he had pulled through for that reason. . . .

Now in the sinking ocean liner, he held the wedge of glass carefully in his hand as though it were some kind of temporary trophy. He tossed it to one side as he went to his knees beside a motionless Becky Houck. No more groans were coming from her, and there was a thin trickle of blood on her forehead.

# Three

Ryan heard the circular metal stairway start to tear away from the floor of the *S. S. Oceanic's* promenade deck. It was a grinding sound that sent sudden chills up and down his spine.

And he saw a terrified Mr. Houck falling back and away from him, muttering something. It sounded like he was saying, "I . . . couldn't hold on to you, Ryan . . . forgive me . . . I just . . . couldn't hold on!"

The stairway, basically one unit, was still attached to the deck beneath him but not tightly. And the motion of the ocean liner that had separated the stairs from the upper level also had weakened the section directly below.

The stairway was wobbling with each new vibration!

Ryan knew that he had to make it either back to the top deck or climb down each step, one by one by one, until he reached the second level. Yet no spot was safe in a sinking ship. At least he assumed it was sinking. Perhaps the explosions had not done enough damage to—.

He started down, deciding that it was too wide a space between the top of the stairway and the main deck.

Smoke.

He smelled smoke.

Ryan's eyes started to water a bit. Then came a hard coughing spell. It was strong enough nearly to tear his fingers from the railing on either side of the metal stairs.

Finally the coughing passed, and he was able to steady himself, his vision soon clearing.

He was halfway down when another more violent explosion abruptly rocked the *S. S. Oceanic.*

He screamed as he was flung from those stairs onto the bare and very hard metal floor of the second level!

Ryan hit the floor with a thud. Pain exploded throughout his body, and he felt himself drifting into unconsciousness. He thought, in a flash, about what had happened earlier:

The suspicious circumstances, just after the S. S. Oceanic *left its dock . . .*

The strange looking man in a large straw hat, with a very wide brim, pulled down over his forehead . . .

Ryan had followed him and saw him entering an isolated part of the engine room of the ocean liner. It was an area where the crew did not go often.

There was something in the man's hands.

Hiding when the man left that almost dark area, Ryan had followed him to other areas of the ship.

Ryan tried to tell a member of the crew, but the officer had been too busy flirting with one of the passengers. The captain wouldn't listen to Ryan either.

Ryan finally located his father and told him what he had seen. Andrew Bartlett believed every word and immediately went to see the captain. A search was begun in the areas where Ryan had seen the strange man. In the first spot, they found a shoe box filled with dirty socks. In another area, they found a box full of equally dirty underwear.

No bombs. Nothing suspicious—odd, yes, but not dangerous.

Decoys! Deliberate fakes!

Ryan realized the truth just as he passed out. *The man had wanted to be spotted. That way when he went around, later, planting the real bombs, nobody would pay attention!*

 # Four

Chad had been able to carry Becky Houck out of the gameroom into the corridor. There were far too many loose objects in the gameroom—billiard balls, cues, other furniture, a couple of video arcade games. They all could become deadly assassins if the ship were set in abrupt motion yet again. There was no way that staying in that room could be justified!

Becky was coming to, whimpering a bit as she moved her arms and legs slightly, painfully.

Chad let out a glad whoop as soon as she opened her eyes and smiled at him.

"What happened?" she said, trying to smile, her voice weak.

"Some kind of explosion," said Chad. "Are you okay?" he asked. "You've got the makings of a big bump on your forehead."

"No concussion," she added, easily anticipating what Chad was thinking. "And I don't have double vision, and I don't feel dizzy."

She smiled, knowing that her level-headed manner was greatly surprising this handsome new friend of hers.

"Are you a nurse or something?" he asked.

"Want to be . . ." she admitted.

Smoke.

"There's a fire somewhere near here," Chad told her. "I think we'd better get out of this area right now.

"I can stand!" Becky said abruptly, proud of herself, testing first her left leg, then the right, feeling surprising strength in both.

"The stairway is—."

Chad was pointing to his left when down the corridor to the right, he saw an elderly woman frantically looking for someone. She stopped in front of the stateroom doors.

"Allen where are you. Allen—" she called out and reached to open the door.

"Don't—!" Chad yelled at her. "If there's a fire on the other—."

She apparently didn't hear what he said or ignored it in a state of panic.

"You just can't do that," Chad shouted again. "You—."

But the woman opened the door anyway, and flames immediately *whooshed* out of the room. She managed to just barely get out of the way and ran screaming down the corridor in the opposite direction.

"Quick, let's get out of here, Becky! Lean on me if you have to," Chad said.

The two of them ran to the left away from the flames. Thankfully, the corridor was paneled in fire-retardant materials.

"Turn left," Chad said. "The stairway is—."

They scurried around a corner. There were the steps just ahead, barely attached to the floor. Their hopes sank when they saw the stairway swinging completely loose from the promenade deck just above them.

"We've got to go another way," Chad said, obviously.

"But the fire . . . it's behind us," Becky added. "We can't turn back. Chad, what do we—?"

"Straight ahead!" he interrupted. *"Now!"*

They hurried to the left of the stairs and almost tripped over a body that was lying face down on the floor.

"It looks like—," he started to say, his heart pounding, hoping that somehow he was very wrong.

Groaning!

Chad saw the body move slightly, then heard a low groaning sound coming from it.

He bent down and gently turned it over.

"Ryan!" he exclaimed, his voice barely below a yell of surprise.

His brother's eyes widened.

"Praise God, it's . . . it's you!" Ryan said.

"Can you stand?" Chad asked.

Ryan sat up slowly.

"I don't think any bones are broken," he replied. "I *think* I can stand. But we can't just *stay* here, broken or not."

He started to stand, with Chad's help.

"I'm okay, except my ankle," Ryan remarked, his face pale. "Must have sprained it in the fall."

"Got to be another way upstairs," Chad said.

"There is," Becky told them. "I know there is at least one more stairway, but . . . but I'm not sure where I . . . I—."

"Don't worry," Chad assured her, trying to sound a lot more certain than he actually felt at that moment. "We'll find it."

In fact, the three of them discovered that locating another stairway, *any* stairway was *not* easy, not easy at all.

That section of the ship was made up entirely of passenger staterooms. Soon the corridors were filled with confused, panic-stricken people.

People were rushing in great fear out of their staterooms, continuing an exodus that had begun immediately after the first explosion. Colliding painfully with one another, many were sent sprawling to the floor, becoming sudden obstacles to those who somehow managed to stay on their feet.

The fire that had started earlier, probably in the huge engine room of the *S. S. Oceanic,* located on the bottom level, was spreading rapidly. It was burning along the complex electrical wiring system, as well as the network of air-conditioning ducts throughout the ship.

These man-made, aluminum air tunnels were proving to be easy pathways for the rapid spread of the searing flames. The spots where the metal surfaces had been joined together were quickly pulling apart and filling with all kinds of combustible material.

The red-hot blaze, which resulted, had burned through all but the most resistant materials on the bottom level of the *S. S. Oceanic,* and now it was beginning to break through on the upper levels.

None of the liner's passengers had any idea if, or when, any of their group would be the next victims engulfed by flames roaring out-of-control!

Five

Andrew Bartlett knew that he didn't have much time left.

The water was rising at a more rapid pace than earlier. It was just an inch below the edge of the bed where he lay trapped.

He could scarcely breathe because of the weight of the twisted metal on him. Periodically he was blacking out, usually for a few seconds but sometimes for a minute or so. And then he would come to again, his head throbbing with a dull ache that made him feel sick to his stomach.

What I need now, Lord, is one of those professional wrestlers on board, he thought, trying to keep his mind going so that he would not pass out. *Somebody like Crusher Malone!*

Ah, Crusher Malone, with the huge biceps and the powerful Boston Crab hold that he applied to all of his losing opponents. . . .

Ryan and Chad both had been thrilled to join their father on an extended Caribbean cruise. But they were even more thrilled when they learned that the *S. S. Oceanic* would be carrying a troupe of well-known professional wrestlers. The wrestlers were on their way to a series of matches on one of the large islands in that region. The island population was quite small, but the TV station there had excellent video facilities. And it was also a chance for the whole pack of experienced wrestlers to have an unofficial vacation at the International Wrestling Federation's expense.

All over the world people watch that stuff, Mr. Bartlett said to himself. *I don't know what they see in it.*

Ryan and Chad were wrestling fans in a big way!

This was understandable in the case of sixteen-year-old Chad. He was a tall, muscular athlete who was one of his school's top amateur wrestlers. He was also a gymnast, as well as a basketball and football star.

But fourteen-year-old Ryan, on the other hand, was usually parked right in front of the extensive computer equipment in his bedroom at home—that is, whenever he happened to have a spare moment, which was almost always. The fact that *he* followed the seemingly outlandish stunts of Crusher Malone, Fahid the Muslim Tyrant, Roaring Randy, Lethal Leonard, and the rest of the members of that band of gypsylike wildmen amazed his father to no end.

If only their mother could see them whooping it up from the audience at the Royal Rumble each year, Andrew Bartlett thought sadly, memories flooding back in on him from an earlier time. *If only . . .*

But she couldn't, of course; she was gone, the victim of a terrorist's bomb that had been rigged to the family car.

Nearly four years ago . . .

Mr. Bartlett was a secret agent for the CIA. But he worked and traveled worldwide in his undercover job as a special envoy for the U. S. State Department. This enabled him to go basically wherever he was needed by the United States Government. But then this, no matter how careful he was, also meant danger—danger not only for himself but for the members of his family as well.

As a result, every few years, the Bartletts had had to pull up their roots and move to a new community somewhere in the United States.

It usually worked.

It usually protected them.

Every so often the enemy tries to track us down, but we've fooled them . . . except that once. Yes, except that one tragic morning, nearly four years ago.

Now he was trapped on a crippled ocean liner which was gradually sinking. Rescue crews had not arrived and no one knew when, or if, they would arrive. But that was not the reason Andrew

Bartlett had been crying. His tears were for a different reason, a different reason entirely.

Six

On the main deck, people were acting as though they were insane with panic. Their craziness heightened with each new lurching movement of the *S. S. Oceanic,* one of the two biggest ocean liners in the world.

Several screamed at the captain, who was trying to direct what was going on in order to prevent as many injuries as possible.

"When are some planes or other ships going to come for us?" one middle-aged man demanded.

"They've been called, sir," replied a nervous young crewman. "I know it's tough, but please, try to be calm."

"Be calm? Is that what you said? Are you out of your mind? We could be dead by the time they get here!"

There aren't enough lifeboats for all of us! What will we do when the ship sinks? I can't swim. How can I help my children? What do we do? Do something . . . please!"

Half of the lifeboats had been destroyed or knocked overboard and sunk as a result of the multiple explosions. Those that remained in their docks couldn't possibly hold all of the passengers since the cruise booking agent had filled every available stateroom.

At the lifeboats, helping to keep back the passengers as much as possible, were two unlikely comrades.

Three-hundred-twenty-pound Crusher Malone and two-hundred-ninety-five-pound Fahid the Muslim Tyrant stood side by side. Vicious opponents in the wrestling ring, now they joined together to help keep order.

"Hope none of our fans can see the two of us now," Malone whispered, his eyes darting from side to side.

"On a cruise ship, with a crowd like this?" Fahid replied. "You got rocks for brains, or something?"

"Hey, who you talking to like that?" Malone said, bristling.

"Cut it out," Fahid barked back. "We're not in the ring now. Forget the act, bozo."

Malone turned red from ear to ear.

"You're right, Bill," he said.

"But don't be *too* friendly, clown!" Fahid/Bill told him.

Malone bit his lip. Fahid the Muslim Tyrant was really Bill Adelman from Texas, but he had a dark, Middle Eastern look that made him perfect for the part. And the way things had been planned to work out in the current series of matches, Fahid would be soundly beaten at the very end, and the crowd would get to its feet and cheer wildly. That was why Adelman went in for it in the first place.

"My Jewish brothers and sisters have been suffering for a long time now at the hands of terrorists," he had said during a serious moment a week or so earlier. "Having the Muslim Tyrant defeated, even if only in wrestling competition, isn't a bad idea at all, not as far as I am concerned!"

Adelman had lost his mother and father near the port city of Haifa, Israel, years before when the packed bus they were on was attacked by two teenagers from a Muslim terrorist organization. Grenades were thrown into the vehicle from both sides. There were no survivors.

Now, in the middle of the Caribbean, on a disabled and gradually sinking ocean liner, Adelman's own life was in danger. Was this, too, an act of terrorists? If terrorists could hijack airplanes and blow them up, what was to keep them from blowing up a cruise ship?

"Life's funny," Adelman told his friend. "I come here to get away from it all, and, presto, look what happens!"

Malone grinned.

"You never can tell, that's for sure," he agreed.

Malone looked out over the main deck. Passengers were in the grip of absolute panic. Their cries mixed together into a kind of common chorus of fear, as more than a hundred men, women, and children stumbled about unsteadily, pushing and shoving toward a limited number of seaworthy lifeboats.

"Cut it out, everybody," Adelman shouted, using his most threatening tone. "This isn't the way to—."

One of the passengers directly in front of him, a blond-haired college football player, reached out and slugged him directly across the jaw.

Adelman smiled.

"You think that hurt, kid?" he yelled triumphantly. "You think I don't get lots worse than that little fly swat in the ring. Look, kid, *this* hurts!"

When he struck back, he used only a fraction of the strength in his broad six-foot-eight frame. But that was enough to send the college student into the air and back down on the deck nearly a dozen feet away.

"Anybody else want to audition for the part of a punching bag?" Adelman asked, snarling.

The crowd quickly calmed down.

Until—.

In just a few minutes, the lifeboats were completely filled with people and were being lowered into the water.

A great many people remained on board, not only the ones on deck, but also many more still below.

The crowd on deck went crazy.

Not even the two wrestlers could stop them. Malone and Adelman were knocked down from the press of all those bodies. People were jumping overboard and trying to climb onto the lifeboats which were still being lowered into the water.

Where are the other guys? Adelman thought as he tried a little uncertainly to get to his feet. *Have they been—?*

He brushed that possibility out of his mind.

Lethal Leonard . . . Roaring Randy . . . oh, Lord, are they gone now? Is this it, Lord?

He wondered, for a moment, how many fans would have paid to see the Muslim Tyrant weeping?

 **Seven**

H ot.

The heat was suffocating.

Chad looked at the other passengers. Everyone was in a corridor that seemed safe, but he knew that it was safe only for the moment. Elsewhere the *S. S. Oceanic* was on fire. It was only a matter of time—whether minutes or an hour or two—before the flames reached them.

Above them was the main deck. Below was another level of staterooms. And below that were the ship's engine rooms.

We could go down, he thought. *Or we could go on up to the deck above us. But how? There are no stairs at either end of this particular corridor, no stairs still attached—.*

When the crowd of them had reached the flight that they had been rushing toward, they found that it too, was no longer attached to the upper deck.

They thought they could get up to the deck by standing on one another's shoulders, and they were about to try that when—.

Another explosion rocked the ship, tossing it from one side to the other.

People were thrown on top of each other. The lights flickered and went off. There were screams of panic.

Finally everyone was able to get to their feet. Ryan, holding a flashlight he had found nearby, tugged at his brother's shirt.

"Chad?" he whispered. "The portal windows—they're oversized. And there are metal railings on the outside of the ship. It's a safety measure."

"How do you know that?" his brother wanted to know.

"I checked out the safety features on the ship before we left home. There's an information service that I can access through my computer's modem hookup."

"You mean everybody can climb out that way? But what about the ones that are hurt or too old?"

Ryan shrugged his shoulders as if to say, *"We do the best we can."*

Again Chad was amazed by his little brother.

Ryan is younger than I am, but sometimes he seems a whole lot older, Chad admitted to himself.

Chad turned and looked again at the scared passengers huddled together in that corridor.

None of them knew what would happen five minutes from then, much less by the next day.

"How many—?" he started to say, not quite sure if he really did have the nerve, his face reddening.

"Yeah, what is it?" a man in his mid forties growled. "You gonna do something to help us, kid?"

The man sounded tough, but Chad could see the awful fear in the man's eyes.

"Sir, would you have any objection if I asked everyone to pray?" Chad said directly to him.

"Pray?" the man repeated, a deep frown on his forehead. "You want us to *pray?*"

Someone else, a thin elderly woman, spoke up as she stepped forward.

"What else do we have, mister?" she said. "We need some guidance, some protection. What's wrong with our praying for that?"

The man hesitated for a moment, then started crying in front of everyone.

"Forgive me," he said. "Please forgive me. I just don't want to die, not now, not here."

Chad walked up to the man.

"Sir, what's your name?" he asked.

"Walter," he replied. 'Walter Coggins."

"I'm not real good with words," Chad said. "If I start to get all tongue-tied, would you jump in and help me?"

"With the prayer?" Coggins asked.

Chad nodded, not quite sure why he had suddenly picked *this* one out of that whole group! And yet, there seemed to be something familiar about the man.

Coggins hesitated, obviously thinking back over memories of long ago.

"I . . . I think . . . I . . . can," he stuttered. "I really think I can. I remember some things, some things from way back."

Chad smiled at him, not sure at all why he—a teenager!—was in charge. Everyone was literally looking in his direction, as though waiting for him to tell them everything to do.

Chad thought, *What would my dad do right now?* He was not sure, but thinking about his dad gave him confidence. He knew praying was the right thing to do—the only thing to do.

"Anyone who can get on their knees, why don't we do that now?" he told them finally. Then Chad and Ryan set the example as they knelt on the floor and bowed their heads.

Everyone followed, doing the same thing, the middle-aged, the elderly, men and women. Ryan, Chad, and Becky were the only young people present. Some had to struggle to keep their balance as the motion of the water outside made them feel like jello in a bowl handled by unsteady hands.

"Lord, we—," Chad hesitated, a tight knot in his throat, "—we are like Jonah in the stomach

36

of the great fish that swallowed him. He didn't die, Lord, but escaped with his life three days later. We've been here only a couple of hours, but it seems like a long time to all of us. Please guide us out of this place, away from danger, if that be Your will. And, Lord, help us to bring honor and glory to Your name whatever happens. We—."

A voice interrupted him, a voice trembling with emotion.

"Father God, we are so weak. Each of us stands before You, condemned, needing Your mercy to flow over us like a cleansing stream."

Chad recognized that voice.

Walter Coggins!

"But that weakness often prevents us from standing before You in confession, in repentance," the man continued. "I have offended You in so many ways, Lord. I . . . I have caused countless numbers to turn away from you because I have pretended to be someone who follows You, but my habits, my actions have spoken otherwise. And now . . . and now—."

Although his own eyes remained closed, Chad could sense that Coggins was standing.

"I can deal with all that, Lord. But I can't stand the . . . the guilt I feel now. It wasn't supposed to be like it's become on this ship. I was . . . supposed to . . . to feel . . . *happy!* That's what that group of fanatical Muslims told me when . . . when—."

Even in the increasing heat of the corridor, Chad felt a sudden cold sensation all along his spine. It started at the base and was working its way quickly up his body. Chad started to realize who this Coggins was.

He nudged Ryan with his elbow.

"I know," his brother whispered. "His name has been in the news for weeks."

Apparently others among the group had made a similar connection.

"You're that man who demonstrated against the war with Iraq," a thinnish man with horn-rimmed glasses said as he got to his feet. "You were about to say something about bombs, weren't you, Mr. Coggins?"

"Yes, *yes!*" the other man yelled in anguish. "*I* planted the explosives. Some guys from Yemen told me what to do. And—and there are . . . more . . . more bombs throughout this ship. *All over the place!*"

"Why did you do this?" the man with the glasses demanded as he closed his hands around the other's neck, choking him. "My wife is probably dead because of you."

Coggins, barely able to talk, tried to explain.

"I did it . . . because . . . because my son died among the sand dunes of Saudi Arabia. He was one of the first casualties of the war in the Middle East. I didn't want the U. S. government to get involved. I made a big thing of this. And I was right. I guess that's why those guys approached me. They knew they would be suspect, but not me.

"Don't you see, I . . . I had to . . . protest and . . . get even! I had to settle . . . the score. Don't you see that? Don't any of you realize that I had no choice? I had to do something big and awful to make a statement! People had to listen to me."

"But why *this* ship?" the other man asked. "It's not a military vessel. Tell me why!"

"It's owned . . . by a German industrialist."

"So what does that prove, mister?"

"Leipziger's the one, you know . . . the same greedy industrialist whose company manufactured some of weapons used by the enemy in the war . . . *that* was how my son died!"

He started laughing, a wicked, cackling laugh that gave a clue as to how insane he had become.

"The bomb that killed him was made by the Leipziger munition plant in Frankfurt!"

"You got involved with a terrorist group to get revenge on a company that makes weapons for them to kill others?" Chad said, stunned by the revelation. "You dealt with the devil in order to murder or maim or cripple innocent people on this ship?"

"Yes, yes, I had to do something, don't you see?" Coggins replied.

39

"But you could die with the rest of us!"

"That doesn't matter. Life doesn't matter. Everyone I love is gone. My wife died of a heart attack, a heart shattered by what happened to our son. What is there to live for? What—?"

Coggins broke the grip on his neck and backed away. The man with the glasses started after him, but Chad stopped him.

"How can he escape?" Chad said. "Where can he go?"

"The fire trapped my wife in our cabin . . . she was taking a nap . . . I had gone upstairs on deck to sit out in the sun, get a tan, then the explosions . . . and . . . and *now*—"

"And so you want to kill him, don't you, sir? You want to get even, just like he did. What's the difference between the two of you then?"

The man hesitated, looking at Chad, then at Coggins who was still backing away, down the corridor, and starting to turn a corner to his left, then disappearing around it.

Seconds passed. No one else was moving.

"Suppose that monster finds some way to save his neck, suppose—," the man said.

Just as he spoke, the *S. S. Oceanic* groaned again, sounding more than ever like a giant dying beast.

"*Look!*" Chad screamed, glancing over his shoulder.

In that instant, Coggins seemed to have been spit out of some invisible mouth, as he was flung backward, past the corner, into view again.

This time he was a victim, hitting the floor hard.

Chad rushed up to the unmoving body, trying to find some indication of a pulse.

Nothing.

Chad turned and faced the others.

"Dead," he told them.

# Eight

Andrew Bartlett could taste the salt water now.

The level was up to his lower lip. He was blacking out more and more frequently, staying conscious less and less often.

"Oh, God, I ask You, please, please, take care of them," he prayed. *"My sons are going to be completely alone. Thank You, Lord, for preparing Chad and Ryan for such a time. What with me on the road so much, the two of them have never truly known if I would make it back to them. And since their mother's death, they realize I could be killed by someone out to get those who do the undercover work that has been mine for more than ten years now."*

Mr. Bartlett felt sick again. His stomach was churning.

"Hold on, there!" the very deep, raspy voice broke into his thoughts. "Hold on another minute or so!"

Mr. Bartlett couldn't turn around because of the way he was pinned down. But he seemed to recognize the voice somehow.

"Who are you, mister?" he asked. "I . . . I know it sounds crazy, but your voice seems familiar."

Whoever he was, he didn't say anything at first. But Mr. Bartlett could hear him groaning with exertion as he got his hands wrapped around the twisted metal and started to pry it back.

"As soon as I say so, mister, can you roll to your left? When I let go, this is going to swing back, and—."

"Yes, yes," Mr. Bartlett assured him. "I think I can."

He could feel the heavy metal being moved off his back.

"*Now!*" the stranger with the familiar voice shouted.

There was some pain, some real pain throughout his body, but Mr. Bartlett *did* manage to roll over twice. In fact, he nearly rolled off the bed altogether but was able to brake himself in time.

The stranger let go a split second later, and the metal swung instantly onto the bed, its impact cushioned by the heavily padded mattress.

Mr. Bartlett turned over, and at last was able to see who his rescuer was.

"Crusher Malone!" he exclaimed as he immediately recognized the wrestling star.

"There when you need me," the giant smiled.

The crowd separated into several different groups. The purpose was to enter separate staterooms and use the oversized portal window in each. Chad started to put his hand on the first doorknob.

He could feel the heat just an inch away.

"Not this one!" he warned. "Fire inside."

A cry of despair shuddered throughout the crowd. The next one was hot as well. And the one after that.

"The other side," Chad told them. "I'll try the other side."

He turned to the left side of the corridor. The first knob was cool to the touch. His fingers closed around it, tried to open the door.

"Locked!" he commented. "We've got to break it in."

"But nobody here is strong enough for that," a man shouted. "We're all up in years. You're a big kid, but those doors are solid. How can you—?"

There was a pause. Then abruptly they heard a loud, deep voice call out.

"I can do it," the voice said. "Piece of cake."

Everyone turned around and looked back down the corridor. A huge man stood there, smiling. He seemed nearly as wide as he was tall.

"Chad, that's—that's—," Ryan stuttered.

"Yeah, I know," his brother agreed. "That's who it is—Fahid the Muslim Tyrant."

"The captain said that I should do whatever I could to help," he told them. "It's so hot down here. I almost went back."

"How did you get down here if we couldn't get up?" Chad asked.

"I just jumped down through the opening where some stairs had been attached," the wrestler replied. "You don't need them to get to this deck, only to climb to the one above it, right?"

Chad nodded, regretting the dumb question.

Adelman/Tyrant went up to the door, braced his upper body against it, and started pushing.

Everyone there could hear metal screeching. In less than a minute, Adelman had torn the door off its hinges.

"We'll need others," Chad told him, still not quite believing that this awful ring villain was helping them. "The south side's hopeless. We have only—."

"Are you Chad Bartlett?" Adelman asked.

"Yes, Fahid, uh, sir! How did you know?"

"Your father told us."

"Dad?" Ryan broke in. "You've seen Dad?"

"Malone got him out of that fix he was in."

"Crusher Malone? The biggest wrestler in the entire business?" Chad asked.

"The one and only," said Fahid.

"And Dad's going to be okay?" Ryan added, scarcely believing what he had just learned.

"At least he won't drown in that cabin," the wrestler answered.

For a moment the two boys forgot themselves and let out one loud whoop of relief. Then they quickly came back down to earth as the other passengers started impatiently to crowd around them.

 # Nine

Dolphins were known to stay together in small-to-large, close-knit family groups. Killer whales, despite their name, were known to do the same thing. Dolphins were able to communicate over a long distance. Scientists and others studying these astonishing creatures continued to be amazed. Dolphins indeed could be many miles apart and yet each still completely aware of what the other was doing.

It was like those old stories involving identical twins, a special link between the two. A thought begun in one is anticipated somehow in the other, as though they were capable of reading one another's minds.

The explosions on the *S. S. Oceanic* sent shock waves through the water. The shocks traveled like sonic booms in the air caused by jet planes, or depth charges sent against enemy submarines in wartime.

A nearby school of dolphins had been caught up in the aftermath. They were severely hurt by the sudden, powerful sound waves underwater.

Some drowned as a result, unable to swim to the surface for precious air. Others, dazed, confused, swam off in several different directions, several against the hull of the *S. S. Oceanic,* fatally injuring themselves, though they did not die instantly. And there were a few which, ultimately, in a weakened state, were eaten by sharks. Some were later caught in fishermen's tuna nets off the coast of one of the Caribbean islands.

Three young dolphins remained at the site where the *S. S. Oceanic* was floundering. They huddled together, their minds stunned into inaction, making them unable to do anything but simply hover uncertainly in the water, comforted, but only to a degree, by one another's company. They were advanced creatures of the deep, yes. But they were not advanced enough to thoroughly reason out what to do in the desperate situation in which the three of them found themselves.

And in the distance, many miles away, the stream of distress calls being sent out by these stranded dolphins was being heard. Even those earlier calls by the ones that had been caught up in the terror of drowning were being picked up.

All these calls were being received by a large school of dolphins on their journey to another place altogether.

. . . Sounds not unlike a baby's cry!

They had no way of knowing the *nature* of the crisis, but that desperate appeal had stirred their instincts as soon as they heard or sensed it. These dolphins understood that some of their kind were in great danger.

So this group of two dozen mammals changed from the direction in which they had been traveling and headed west toward the *S. S. Oceanic* instead.

The distress signals they had heard apparently were not only from their own kind.

Other sounds. Human sounds. . . .

Sounds they had heard many times as they swam near jetties of rock jutting out into the ocean. Often they saw humans standing there, looking at them, sometimes throwing food out to them.

Once there had been a child that had slipped on one section of the rocks, and tumbled into the surf, and was sucked out further into the ocean by a vicious undertow.

Strong men quickly dived into the water and tried to grab him, but they could not reach the child because of the strong current.

Two dolphins had been nearby.

They saw the tiny form sink helplessly below the foaming surface of the water.

And they reacted. But this was not the first time such a thing had happened. There had been many instances where their kind had saved humans from drowning, from sharks, from other calamities.

One of them managed to get under the child, stopping him from sinking any further. The other grabbed his body gently in its snout and took him back to the surface. That dolphin then let go and was joined by the other one. The two of them floated the child on the surface until a human was only inches away.

Among the humans, this rescue had been something that was talked about well into the night. Though, when they researched such a thing, they would realize that it had happened before. There were reports of such rescues in the Pacific Ocean dating back nearly fifty years.

Now a school of dolphins was on its way to the *S. S. Oceanic*. They began their rescue mission when they heard the calls of their own kind. But they would not limit their attempts at helping to just other dolphins.

Perhaps, though intelligent, they simply were responding because of some natural ability to *sense* fear, whether from human beings or sea mammals like themselves.

Whatever the case, only one thing sent them to that site, that place of terror.

There were calls, calls for help, and they needed nothing else to send them on their way.

Ten

One by one, the passengers were able to crawl out through the oversized portal windows and grab the metal railings on the side of the S. S. Oceanic. For the younger ones, and there were only a few of these, the climb up to the promenade deck was not so difficult.

For the other passengers, it was another story altogether.

Adelman/Tyrant couldn't get through the portal because it just wasn't big enough for his huge body, so he wasn't able to go ahead of the passengers and help them up the railings.

Of the remaining passengers, only Chad was strong enough to do that.

Not again! Chad thought. Yes, *Lord, I know all about suffering trials and tribulations, and the fact that we have to be prepared to face these, but, please, couldn't You let up for a while?*

Chad wondered about Ryan being the first passenger to go out through the portal. He looked quickly and, he hoped, not too obviously at the people waiting in that cabin and outside in the corridor.

Ryan could go by himself. He's a little shrimp, yeah, but his size and lack of weight are in his favor this time around. My little brother could scamper up the side like a little monkey.

And yet—.

He knew what would happen if his brother went ahead of everyone else. People would be shouting unpleasant comments at him for showing favoritism. And their language would be rough, to put it mildly.

And they might panic. Anger and panic are not a great combination. It might mean a riot. What do I do?

None of this thinking took more than a few seconds. He didn't have any time to spare.

Ryan made the decision an easier one.

"Go ahead," his little brother said. "It's okay. You don't have much of a choice."

"Did you read my—?" Chad started to say, deeply proud of this scrawny little computer nut.

"I just know you. And I love you whatever happens, bro."

It was funny that Ryan chose *bro,* a term he himself used to say before it went hopelessly out-of-date with his friends.

"All right, everybody," Chad said as he started to push himself through the portal. "Mr. . . . Mr., uh—."

He wasn't sure how to address the Muslim Tyrant.

"Bill," Adelman told him. "This really isn't stage time now, no faked crisis here. Yeah, just call me Bill."

"Okay, Bill, when I call down, start sending them up."

"You got it, bro!"

Chad smiled briefly, realizing that his brother didn't have the only claim on that term. Even in the danger of that moment, Chad had to admit that he was still thrilled that someone like this power-house wrestler would actually use it to refer to *him*!

The railings wouldn't have helped anybody as big as Bill, Chad realized. They were hardly adequate for his much smaller hands.

He climbed three railings up, then stopped. Turning around, he looked toward the portal window.

An elderly woman was being helped through. Maintaining a grip on the nearest railing just above his head, he reached down and took her hand as gently as he knew how.

For an instant their eyes seemed to meet. She flashed a somewhat nervous smile at him.

"Praise God for His goodness in having you here, son," she said, her old voice barely loud enough to hear.

Chad smiled back at her and then climbed up the set of railings one by one, the old woman's hand in his own. With her other hand she grabbed hold of each railing at her level.

Mercifully, the S. S. *Oceanic* didn't heave or shudder or roll more than slightly. They were able to reach the promenade deck as quickly as anyone could have hoped. Somebody had spotted what was going on and alerted the crew.

Captain Henricksen himself was directly above them, reaching down, his own strong hand taking Chad's. Then the two of them reached down and helped the woman over the edge and onto the deck.

She was shaking badly, her wrinkled face creased even more as she tried to get her breath.

She saw them looking at her with great concern.

"This isn't out of fear," she hastened to to tell the two of them. "The Lord wouldn't be honored by that. My body is shaking now because I've not had to go through that kind of exercise for a very long time. And I'm just not accustomed to it anymore."

"Bless you," Chad said as he hurried to the edge and started back down toward the portal.

Captain Henricksen—a tall, blond, broad-shouldered, Swede—called to him. "Can you do this again and again, young man? Unfortunately I have no crew members to spare. The passengers here on the deck are frantic. I don't know how much longer we can keep the people calm. The situation is nearly out of control."

He lowered his voice as he added, "It's not going to be easy."

Chad's expression indicated that he understood, and he added, "It's okay, sir. I've got Someone by my side every minute."

Henricksen paused a moment, then wiped his eyes with the back of his left hand. He looked a little embarrassed as he did so, as though this showed some kind of weakness.

"So do I, my young friend. You see, I could never *hope* to get through this otherwise."

Chad nodded in agreement and then clambered as quickly as he could back to the portal window directly below. One by one he helped the women first, then the men.

Eleven

Chad saw a group of fins not more than a few hundred yards from the *S. S. Oceanic.*

Sharks!

Just then a rather short man who was making his way up the ship lost his grip and nearly fell. Chad grabbed the man's arm just in time.

"Thank You, Lord," the shaken teenager said. "Thank You for helping me get him to safety."

"Safety . . ." He repeated that word a couple of times, not sure if it meant anything. After all, getting back to the main deck of the ship was only part of the problem facing the passengers below.

Where was any hint of a rescue effort that must surely be on the way? How much longer would it take for—?

He swallowed several times in a row as one terrible thought entered his mind.

Does anyone on the outside even . . . know?

Perhaps the ship's short wave transmissions had been so damaged by the different explosions that no SOS message had ever gotten out in the first place.

Could it be that there won't be any help?

He saw that his hands were trembling. He couldn't let the others know that he was shook up. Suddenly now it seemed ridiculous after everything that he had been through thus far.

He had to be strong. Too many people were depending on him. He had to—.

Once again Chad looked down at the group of fins in the water below him.

Dolphins!

Chad squinted, examining them a bit more carefully.

Of course! Not sharks at all. Shark fins were broader, blunter, not quite as curved as these were.

Chad had often thought that, someday, he might investigate going into marine biology as a career. He knew he couldn't possibly make much of a career for himself by being a jock all his life.

Still, working as a marine biologist would let him use many of his athletic skills. Besides, he felt especially drawn to the mammals of the world's oceans. However, his brother was even more interested in them.

Ryan had picked up on their intelligence right away, Chad thought. *He noticed immediately the way those large creatures communicate with one another, the rapport they seem to feel with any human being who treats them with a little kindness.*

Chad started to perspire as he remembered some intense studying his genius brother had helped him with. The two of them had gone to the library to do research for a term paper. They had found some fascinating material. It told how dolphins were being treated in their natural habitats, far away from safe little zoos and special aquariums.

The truth the two of them pieced together was harsh, very harsh: When not sheltered by caring individuals, dolphins almost always faced cruel treatment on the part of certain insensitive human beings. It seemed that some people just couldn't care less about the specialness of this group of mammals.

Chad remember how angry he had gotten when he learned how dolphins are mistreated. He and Ryan had sat, disbelieving at first, watching video scenes of hundreds of dolphins caught in tuna nets. Their strange little cries had filled the air, sounding a little like *"Help us! Help us! Help us!"*

How callously their bodies were cast overboard. The only worthwhile "catch" was the tuna, which was a high profit item for the fishermen. The interest of these men seemed centered in their pocketbooks, regardless of the harm consistently done to innocent creatures such as the dolphins!

 # Twelve

One by one the passengers were able to make it up the row of railings to the top deck. There were no more mishaps.

Then it was Ryan's turn.

Adelman/Tyrant lifted him up to the round window, and pushed him out as far as possible. Ryan reached directly above his head and grabbed the first white metal railing. His fingers, actually quite small for his age, wrapped easily around it.

That hadn't been the case for all of the other passengers.

Most found holding on to the railings to be awkward business. More than one nearly fell to their deaths.

For Ryan, it needn't have been tough at all. He was short, weighed just over a hundred pounds, and climbing the railings should never have presented any problems.

Except for one thing.

Another bomb.

And the most powerful yet.

Ryan struggled to hold to the railing, thoughts of the huge whale in the movie version of *Moby Dick* rushing into his mind. When the ancient creature was being harpooned by the mad Captain Ahab, it reared up defiantly, letting out a dying cry, just before plunging to its doom.

The *S. S. Oceanic* sounded like some sort of metal, plastic, and glass super beast. No longer able to hold on to any kind of mechanical life, the starboard end dipped suddenly. It began, at last, to submit mournfully to a cold and dreary death.

What had been a truly majestic vessel less than three hours earlier was now torn and twisted, and quite ugly. The *Oceanic* was a tragic sight.

People were screaming wildly, a dozen of them knocked off balance and sent slipping nearly over the side and into the water. Their eyes were wide and bloodshot and terrified.

And Ryan!

His brother's hand reached down toward him, the two groping frantically in mid air toward one another, fingers only a bare few inches apart.

And then Ryan was torn from the railings, as he had been from the stairway earlier. He was plunged head first into the turquoise-colored water, so clear, yet so deadly. *And Ryan could not be seen coming up to the surface again!*

Thirteen

Ryan had come close to drowning once or twice before in his adventure-filled life. Not being able to breathe, then as now, was a kind of ultimate nightmare. Very little could be compared with it . . . *the frightful feeling of utter helplessness . . . mouthfuls of water pouring into his lungs . . . needing air . . . trying not to take in water where air used to be accepted so routinely.*

Those other times someone had been nearby and had pulled him back to the surface. They had either taken him back to land or put him on some sort of boat. Immediately someone had pressed downward on his chest until he started coughing up the water in violent spasms.

Not this time. There were plenty of people around, but most of *them* were fighting for their own survival.

Ryan's last mental picture was of the Muslim Tyrant framed in that portal window, shouting at him . . . then immediately bursting into tears when his own helplessness was apparent.

Ryan's eyes were stinging as much from patches of oil in the water as from the salt content. He tried to keep them closed.

"Chad!" he cried. "Chad, I'm dying, I'm—!"

His brother didn't seem to be anywhere around. Ryan sank below the surface for the third time.

When that happens, you're as good as dead. . . .

The terror gave way to a surprising peace, a feeling of joy spreading through his entire body.

"Lord, I'm ready!" he exclaimed. *"But I'm scared. Let me feel Your hand in mine . . . please!"*

Like anybody who is only fourteen years old, Ryan had seldom had to consider what it would be like for him to die. That was an event that probably awaited him fifty or sixty or seventy years into the future—too far into the future to let it bother him anytime soon.

There had been more than one occasion over the years when death seemed *close,* yes. That was a fact of life for a family such as the Bartletts, what with the international intrigue that was a daily part of Andrew Bartlett's job. And, of course, there was always the spillover into his father's private life.

But never before, in all that had happened had Ryan seemed to be actually experiencing death *itself!*

In his mind he was beginning to whisper good-bye to his father, his brother Chad, to friends in school when—.

An instant later, something smooth, almost rubbery in its feel touched his left hand, then his right.

Ryan closed all the fingers of both hands around it, or tried to do so. But they slid off at first, as though the surface of whatever it was had been greased and was now very, very slippery. He tried again. Within seconds he had managed to establish a firm hand on it. He thought of the slippery, inflated toy duck he had had as a small child.

And he felt himself moving. Moving, yes, but not down.

Up, up real fast, the water heavy against his face.

Ryan's eyes remained closed. He felt he *couldn't* open them just then.

The pounding. Worse at his forehead!

My head! he screamed to himself. *My head's going to burst, and . . . and nobody will ever find what's left of me. How COULD they ever find me? I'm so small and the ocean's just too big for—!*

Like some kind of life raft, his mind wrapped around memories of his mother. She'd been the one who had taught him to swim because his father happened to be off as usual in a foreign country, doing what he had to do. But Andrew Bartlett was aware of the strain his long trips sometimes caused at home. And he always tried to make up for it when they were all together.

Mom was so beautiful, Ryan remembered. *She seemed able to smile about almost anything.*

There was only pain frozen on her face that morning after her body had been thrown from the family car by an explosion. The bomb had been traced to a terrorist group that wanted to get back at—.

Dad! He realized that one of his prayers had been answered, that his father had escaped drowning on the ship.

Rescued by a pro wrestler!

Ordinarily Ryan would have smiled at anything like that.

But now Chad and my father are back on the ship, maybe safe for a while, and I'm here—.

He felt something brush against his cheek briefly, like the touch of a single feather!

And he moved his hand to his cheek, only to discover that it was a slight breeze that had done so.

A breeze that he felt because he was now—!

Above the surface of the water, poking his head through a layer of foam, and looking up at the cloudless blue sky. His eyes opened wide, his very soul rejoicing. And he realized that he was being carried *forward!*

Two fins pierced the water on either side of him. One full-sized dolphin had been *moving* him along. Another had been swimming just below, as though to catch him if he had slipped off. Their bodies were so close together that they nearly touched, as though they both were physically linked in some way.

The reality of that was stunning.

There have been reports for years that dolphins have saved people from sharks. But I don't remember anything like this. I—.

He turned his head slightly, and saw several other pairs of fins to his left. Floating between *them* were the three other dolphins that had been severely affected by the explosions on board the *S. S. Oceanic*. They were obviously injured and were making pathetic little mewing sounds, like injured kittens.

Dolphins beach themselves every so often, Ryan thought. *Once there was a telecast of some people who got one of them back into the ocean. Others of its kind floated it on the surface for as long as they could, but it died anyway. There's not much known about why they seem to commit a form of suicide.*

All were heading toward a faint form in the distance, something that looked like land. Or was it just the ragged look of where clouds and water come together.

Ryan realized suddenly that he had been holding with both hands onto the fin of the dolphin supporting his weight on its back. He closed his fingers more tightly around it as he recognized what that mist-covered form directly ahead of him really was.

An island in the middle of that stretch of ocean!

Fourteen

Bill Adelman/Fahid the Muslim Tyrant was trapped. He knew it. There was no way he could get through the portal window.

He ran out into the corridor.

The temperature had risen. It felt like a very humid summer afternoon in Houston, and that was about as hot as he had ever experienced. But it surely would get a great deal hotter as more of the *S. S. Oceanic* actually caught fire. And the flames continued to increase by the minute, spreading to more and more staterooms.

I have no place to go. . . .

That thought caused a cold chill to race up and down his spine, despite the scorching heat.

It must be a little like Hell.

Adelman sank down to his knees. He hadn't thought much about Hell over the years. There was too much about life on earth that seemed to fit some descriptions he'd heard when he was changing channels in a motel room on Sundays while he was on the road.

And yet—he prayed.

I'm trapped. Oh, God—.

He cut himself off.

It's been a long time.

Admitting that to himself was very awkward. So much of his life had been spent in a way that he knew was not earning him "any eternal credits," as he once had put his feelings in the matter.

Besides, I'm Jewish. What do I need to know about the New Testament or stuff like that?

His eyes closed briefly, his head pounding, as he leaned back against the metal wall.

He expected never to open them again. He expected simply to go to sleep and cease to exist, or to drift off into some world of clouds and mist and strange spirits.

And nothing will be left of my body but a pile of ashes in a huge coffin at the bottom of the Atlantic Ocean!

His eyes shot open.

No!

He'd heard a sound. Not far away. At least it didn't seem to be far.

To the contrary, it seemed *so close!*

What a Friend we have . . .

A tiny voice. Hardly loud enough to hear.

How can I be hearing it? It sounds like—

Yes! Yes, it did. It did sound like a—.

. . . all our sins and griefs to bear.

A child! A child was singing.

Where is she? he thought frantically. *Show me where—!*

He got to his feet, then stopped for a moment.

Who am I talking to? Who is going to show me?

The voice seemed to be getting a little weaker.

Precious Savior . . .

Over there—to his left! From one of the staterooms! The door was slightly ajar. That tiny, tiny voice seemed to be coming from within.

He staggered as he tried to walk. The heat had intensified. Suddenly, just behind him, one of the other stateroom doors *blew open!* Flames leapt out into the corridor.

He could feel the ends of the hair on back of his neck being singed, accompanied by a *sizz-sizz-sizz.* It was a sound like bugs hitting one of those special flourescent-type lamps designed to keep them away from an outdoor barbecue or a swim party.

His mind seemed to explode with pain.

"No!" he declared. "No, I . . . I can't give up. I must save that child. I must do that before . . . before—!"

He didn't want to say out loud what surely he knew, what surely he knew deep down in his gut.

I'm a goner. I'm a—. But not that child. Not—.

Adelman stood in the doorway leading into the stateroom and saw her immediately. She was crouched in a corner, holding a little ragdoll. She looked up just then and saw him as well.

"Jesus !" she cried in relief. "Thank you, Jesus. Thank you, Lord."

"No, child," he tried to tell her. "I'm not—."

She smiled.

"Then you're an angel. Jesus sent an angel to help me."

"I . . . I'm not—," he stuttered.

She jumped to her feet.

"Then you're a friend!" she said confidently.

She rushed up to him, and put her little arms around his leg, and hugged him tightly.

"Jesus knows . . ." she started to sing from the same old hymn.

He bent down and took her up in his arms.

"Sing with me," she asked him.

"I don't know the words, girl," he told her.

"I'll teach you," she assured him.

"We don't have time, child."

"My name isn't child or girl. It's Julie. And we should *always* have time for Jesus, you know. He's our Savior and . . . and—."

"He's not my—," he started to say.

She put her fingers on his lips.

"Shush," she said, her smile broader than ever, and returned to singing more of that hymn.

"Oh, what peace . . ." she went on, her voice out of key but—.

He looked at her sweet, trusting face.

I've never seen such . . . trust. I've never known any myself. And yet here she is, on a ship, doomed, with fire all around us, and she's—.

Trusting.

Tears streamed down his cheeks.

"Forgive me," he said, not intending to say anything out loud, but the words were spoken just the same.

"Why?"

"I feel so weak."

"It doesn't matter, mister. Jesus is our strength. He just takes over, you know. He gives us all we need."

She touched one of the teardrops with her thumb.

"Be happy," she told him. "He's promised never to forsake us, never to leave us, mister. He's . . . He's with us forever."

Just then there was a roaring sound out in the corridor. He hurried to the doorway, the little girl in his arms.

A ball of flame was rushing down the corridor.

"Oh, God!" he cried.

"Jesus will—,"

"Quiet, Julie, *please!*"

"Jesus will—," she continued patiently, with complete trust.

He slammed shut the door to the stateroom. The portal window! That was the only way. He put the little girl gently down on the floor and rushed to the window, pulling the frame away to expose the same opening as in the other stateroom. He stuck his head out, screaming more loudly than he had ever done during any professional wrestling match.

No one responded. There was too much noise and confusion on the main deck.

Other screams. People panicked. Cries of pain.

"Turn your eyes upon Jesus," Julie had started to sing with a joy that seemed to flow from every part of her body. "Look full in His—."

He withdrew, for a moment, from the portal window and turned slowly to his little companion.

"You really believe that, don't you?" he asked her.

"Oh, I do, oh, I do," she said excitedly. "I really do. Jesus is—."

He fell to his knees in front of her.

"Teach me, child," he begged. "I really want to learn about what it is that you believe."

"My *name* is Julie," she said.

"Teach me to believe and to pray, Julie," he added. "Will you please help me to do that?"

"Close your eyes," she said simply.

He did.

"Now ask Jesus to forgive your sins and tell Him that you accept Him as your Savior."

He fumbled with the words, then managed to speak them slowly, awkwardly. He felt very strange saying those words of trust in Jesus, but he truly did believe.

Fingers touched his forehead.

"Oh, Julie," he sobbed. "Oh, Julie, I really mean it. I feel so—."

And he did. He felt so calm all of a sudden. The heat didn't matter. The rocking motion of the ship, a faint background moaning of metal and other materials in a kind of dying gasp . . . *didn't matter*.

Turn your eyes upon Jesus . . . he thought.

That was what mattered. More than any escape. More than—.

"So beautiful, Julie," he said, the tears coming nonstop at that point. Their salty taste was really strong as they dripped over the edge of his upper lip and into his mouth.

He felt that gentle touch once again on his forehead, soft, tender. He reached out to take that hand in his own, opening his eyes again, his vision never clearer, his emotions never calmer.

Look full in—His wonderful face.

And he did.

The Muslim Tyrant did.

Fifteen

Rescue! Another vessel could be seen on the horizon, heading toward the sinking ocean liner. It seemed big enough to be a battleship!

Everyone on the main deck also looked up at the clear sky as they heard the sound of approaching helicopters. Three of the giant man-made "birds" were now almost directly overhead.

"Praise God!" a rather plump young woman standing to Chad's left shouted with relief.

Andrew Bartlett was on Chad's other side, his left hand resting gently on his son's right shoulder.

"Ryan is gone, Dad," Chad said with great despair in his voice. "Ryan is really gone."

His father could barely hold back his own sorrow. He hadn't been able even to *try* to help Ryan. Once again he was nowhere near someone he loved when they desperately needed him—even though the three of them had taken this trip in order to be together.

"How are we going to get along without him?" Chad started to say. "How can we ever—?"

Finally any other words choked up inside him. And he stopped talking altogether. The thought of losing his brother hurt too much.

Crusher Malone was standing to one side. Chad could see that he was talking with Becky and her father, and he overheard some of what was being said.

"They're all gone," Malone muttered. "I'm the only one left. All of them wiped out!"

"I know . . ." Becky said. "I feel for Chad and his father, too. I've lost no one. Dad and I are still together."

She reached out and took her father's hand in her own.

"I know how I'd feel if it were you who—," she added, but could not continue.

Andrew Bartlett heard this as well.

"Chad?" he said as he glanced at his son.

Knowing instinctively what he meant, Chad nodded. The two of them walked over to the little group.

Crusher Malone acted like a frightened over-sized child, not at all sure of where to turn next.

"We were friends," Malone said as he saw Chad and Andrew Bartlett standing in front of him, "buddies for a lot of years. The others, too. I loved every one of them. And now . . . and now—."

The five of them hugged one another in that sad moment of shared grief.

Sixteen

Those two dolphins that had been with Ryan were no longer swimming close together, supporting him. He was left to struggle to shore on his own. They had split apart, however, only when both had come as close to that stretch of land as they dared to do so, without being in danger of beaching themselves.

Some fragment of memory poked its way up into the conscious part of Ryan's mind, a fragment that took him back to Sea Life Park on the island of Oahu, Hawaii. He remembered the large aquarium tank with various trained seal, penguin, killer whale, and dolphin acts.

One performance there had involved two of the prized dolphins and their female trainer. Ryan had paid attention to the dolphins while Chad seemed hypnotized by the trainer. Just as Ryan himself was now being balanced between two of them, so was she with the two large ones at that aquarium.

After the performance was over, he was able to spend a few minutes with the trainer, with Chad eagerly tagging along.

Her name was Cindy Farnsworth.

"They're actually trainable to do just about anything that they can *physically* accomplish," she told them. "In fact, once there is a bonding between a human being and one or more of the dolphins, well, it's like a marriage. They seem to take to it naturally."

"But how do you explain this?" Ryan asked.

"I don't know *scientifically*," she offered. "I think sometimes they are a leftover from Eden."

Ryan's eyes lit up. Chad's had been that way ever since he shook hands with Cindy!

"You're a Christian!" Ryan exclaimed.

"You bet I am," she replied happily. "And I have a theory that I think goes along with Scripture."

"Tell us," Ryan said eagerly.

"I believe that part of what was lost when Adam and Eve sinned, and were kicked out of Eden, was their ability to communicate with the rest of God's creation. And I *mean* communicate in the fullest sense of that word—understanding each other, taking part together, talking. There was no death, which meant that lions and lambs were not enemies. At least one creature, the serpent, talked!"

"And dolphins give a hint, just a hint, of what it must have been like in Eden," Ryan said. "Is that it, Cindy?"

"It's only a guess," she admitted. "But if you spent as much time with dolphins as I do, you'd really begin to wonder about that sort of thing . . . you really would."

Back to the present . . .

Weakened from the ordeal he had just been through, Ryan collapsed on shore, vomiting. Not much remained on his stomach from an early breakfast on the *S. S. Oceanic* with his dad and his brother. It was the last time the three of them had been together. Shortly afterward the bombs on board had started exploding.

He was now very weak from the emotional strain as well as the physical ordeal.

Chad! And Dad! Did a rescue ship or helicopter or whatever come in time? I wish I could tell you both what happened to me!

But how?

That question gnawed at him.

Yet, as far as Chad was concerned, Ryan had sunk below the surface of the Atlantic Ocean and hadn't come back.

How could Chad, or anyone else, for that matter, have guessed that Ryan had been pulled away from the ship by a strong undertow and been rescued by a group of dolphins?

Ryan thought about that for a moment as he rested against the warm white sand.

How could they have known? How was anything that had happened to him during the past few minutes, or however long it was, even remotely possible?

Ryan remembered having heard a number of documented, true stories about humans being rescued by dolphins. During World War II, at the Pacific war front, dolphins had saved soldiers fighting for their lives after their boats had been sunk by enemy fire.

It wasn't against the Japanese that they were fighting in those instances but, rather, marauding sharks. Many soldiers died, but many more were saved by large masses of dolphins which had sped to the scene. In each case, the dolphins had beaten off the usually larger, man-eating sharks. Countless numbers actually had been killed by the dolphins.

But most of the time, that wasn't the end of it. The dolphins didn't simply do this one job and then swim off, having performed their Good Samaritan deeds and that was that. They *assisted* the surviving soldiers to the nearest island or to the mainland, wherever that happened to be.

There was just too much other evidence about the capabilities of dolphins, and to Ryan, it was all fascinating. But the story that affected him most deeply was one that had occurred at the scene of a tuna fishing fleet's daily catch. As usual, the nets entangled a great many helpless dolphins, all of which died agonizing deaths of outright suffocation.

One of the crew of fishermen, tripped by a net, happened to fall overboard.

The fisherman was being attacked by a particularly large shark. And he had already been badly bitten when, out of nowhere, a dolphin came charging through the water, hitting the shark with its long, tough snout.

At first the shark did not know what had hit it. But it was distracted long enough for crew members to throw a line to their comrade and get him back on board that particular ship.

The dolphin wasn't so fortunate.

Normally these mammals work together as a team. But that particular group had been nearly wiped out by the fishing fleet, and this single dolphin seemed to be the only one left. Though completely alone, it acted anyway.

After recovering, the shark turned on the dolphin and cut it to ribbons in less than a minute. Then the shark swam off somewhere else, leaving the men on all the ships in that fleet looking on in amazement at what had happened.

With their nets, the fishermen had been responsible for killing nearly two hundred of the dolphins. Yet one of those very creatures had rescued a helpless human being who was a party to the actual slaughter!

The prow, the front, of the *S. S. Oceanic* was visible above the water, but not much more than that.

"They'd better hurry," Andrew Bartlett said nervously as the helicopter hovered over that area.

Chad nodded, realizing how correct his father was.

They were the last ones to leave the ship. Mr. Bartlett's connections at the highest level of government meant that he could ask for whatever he wanted during the rescue period. And what he and his son wanted was to remain in that area as long as possible on the chance that they would learn something positive about Ryan, something that would be an answer to prayer.

Crusher Malone asked if he could stay with them. Mr. Bartlett agreed without hesitation.

They'd better hurry. . . .

Divers had gone deep into the ocean liner's submerged section, hoping to find survivors, passengers caught in pockets of air that had temporarily saved them from drowning.

It's happened before, hours later, after ships have been on the ocean floor. It's not unusual.

That was how Mr. Bartlett had tried to comfort Malone. And it had given the wrestler the slightest hope that some of his friends might still be alive, struggling, yes, perhaps close to suffocation, but still—.

The divers would have to exit the ship any minute.

Very soon the *S. S. Oceanic* would begin its final slide down into the water, disappearing forever, and them with it if they stayed too long.

Seventeen

ahid the Muslim Tyrant/Bill Adelman had been praying silently for a long time. He couldn't guess how much time had passed, but it seemed like most of his life had been relived, incident by incident, as the air in the stateroom got thinner and thinner.

I'm ready, Lord. I'm really ready. . . .

He smiled at the little girl as she snuggled up close to him, one hand on his arm, the other holding her battered doll.

Thank you, darling child. Thank you for helping me to believe, to trust. Thank God for bringing us together.

He glanced at her face. The expression on it was one of utter calm, of complete confidence. Little Julie showed no fear, no nervousness, which Adelman found astonishing.

When peace, like a river, attendeth my way . . .

She had been humming the melody that went

with those words, and he'd asked her if she knew them. She said that she did and repeated them for him.

Oh, Lord, he thought, *to know that peace, to know it now, when—.*

"There is something else," the little girl said.

"What's that, Julie?"

She repeated a verse from the New Testament: *I have learned the secret of being happy at any time in everything that happens.*

"Even here, dear child?" Adelman asked, not sure that he could go as far as that.

She nodded enthusiastically.

"If I only could, if only—," he said, struggling with the idea, so simple yet so hard to understand. How could he be *content* in an air pocket in a cruise ship that would probably prove to be a gigantic metallic coffin for the two of them, and soon, too?

Her hand tightened on his arm. Her face took on the look of special pleading, an urgency it was impossible to ignore. And she said only a single word then. She said, simply, "Please. . . ."

Yes!

In a sudden burst of emotion, he knew he could make that leap of faith, going from faith to trust to contentment.

"Yes!" he said out loud. "Oh, yes, I *can*, blessed child. I *can* do what you say!"

Less than a minute later, one of the divers found him.

In a stateroom into which an air hole somehow had been sucked.

There he was, in the far corner, a three-hundred-pound giant of a man clutching a child's battered doll.

Humming *It is Well with My Soul.*
Alone.

Eighteen

Ryan saw a remarkable but very sad sight directly in front of him.

The injured dolphins had beached themselves, the three of them near death there on the sand.

But the healthy dolphins lingered out in the water, staying nearby, and sticking their snouts upward as they opened their mouths and let out a strange and mournful cry.

I can't let this happen, Lord, but I'm so puny, Ryan thought. *How can I drag even one of them out into the ocean? How can—?*

But he told himself that he had to try. He knew he could not just stand and watch—not after knowing that dolphins had been responsible for saving his life.

He hurried over to one of the three on shore. The top and bottom part of its snout was opening and closing, opening and closing, the hole on top of its head moving as well, sucking in, then out, in, then out.

Ryan touched the dolphin gently just above its eyes from which water was trickling.

Are you crying? he said to himself, then decided it was foolish to think that this mammal was quite as human as that.

He put his arms around the tail and pulled with all the strength he had left. Again and again and again he pulled.

The creature could not be budged.

Ryan looked frantically at the two others. One of them seemed a little smaller. He rushed up to it and tried to pull it back into the water, at least far enough so that it could float, making it easier for the others to—.

Not an inch.

If only I had Chad's muscles, if only I had gotten into gymnastics like he did, then maybe I could do something.

A gasping sound started coming from the smaller of the three dolphins.

Suddenly its tail started to twitch in a frantic manner.

Oh, Lord, help him, please, please help him!

The dolphin actually managed to turn itself around toward the ocean after facing, as were the others, toward land.

Ryan stood by helplessly, though, as the dolphin suddenly stopped moving altogether. It seemed to be looking one last, sad time at the water—at the foam-crested waves breaking only a few yards away. Then, after a few short seconds, it let out a sigh that could barely be heard. Its sides collapsed inward, its eyes closing, the snout frozen in a slightly open position. . . .

Ryan threw back his head and let out one great cry of sorrow.

The divers had brought up Adelman/the Muslim Tyrant safely and put him on the helicopter that also held Andrew and Chad Bartlett, as well as Crusher Malone and Becky Houck and her father.

"Praise God! Praise God! Praise God!" Malone kept saying at first, then stopped. Blushing, he added, "I'm sorry, Bill. I know how you feel about such things."

"No, you don't," Adelman told him. "Not since—."

And he started to tell them all about what had happened—about Julie, the sweet child who helped him see Jesus.

"What happened to her?" asked Chad. "Who was she?"

"I don't know; she just disappeared. Maybe she was an angel."

Just then a message came in on the helicopter communications system.

"We've sighted a teenage boy on an island less than five miles from here! We will land immediately

99

and keep you informed."

Andrew Bartlett spoke up.

"Don't wait," he ordered the pilot. "Get the location and head there right now."

"Will do," the pilot replied.

"But, Dad," Chad said, "if it's Ryan, how did he get that far away from here? He's never been a good swimmer!"

As the helicopter headed in the direction given over the shortwave radio, Mr. Bartlett and Chad looked at one another and bowed their heads in prayer.

They were not alone in doing that.

Nineteen

Ryan heard a helicopter coming closer and closer just as he sank to his knees in exhaustion. The other two dolphins were still alive as far as he could tell, but that would not be so if they stayed on the beach much longer.

He turned and, incredibly, saw more fins than he could count still swimming together just beyond the beach, other dolphins having joined the original group. The sound of their sorrowful cries periodically carried to shore.

They're waiting, he thought. *Oh, Lord, how could they ever know what's going on? What wisdom have You allowed to remain with them, after all these years?*

Ryan stood, waving his hands, hoping that whoever it was on the helicopter had seen him.

In a couple of minutes, the large "bird" had landed a few hundred yards away, the whirling of its blades stirring up a mini sandstorm that quickly ended as the motor wound down.

Two strangers hurried over to him, two very large men, their faces wrinkled up with concern.

They extended their hands and introduced themselves as Randy Mitchell and Kyle Gregg.

"Are you Ryan Bartlett?" Mitchell asked.

"I am," he replied, holding his breath for a moment as he half expected them to tell him some awful news about his father and his brother. "Are my dad and Chad . . . are they okay?"

Gregg smiled as he said, "A Number One, considering all that happened back there"

"Help me, please," Ryan said frantically. "Everything you've said is wonderful, but . . . but these dolphins will die if we don't get them back into the water."

"Look!" Mitchell said. "Look out there!"

The remaining dolphins were acting more excitedly, jumping high out of the water, then splashing back down.

"And there!" Ryan said, pointing to the two that were now just barely alive. "Listen to them!"

They were making mewing sounds, like baby kittens, and their tails were flapping back and forth on the sand.

"It's as though they know something is going on," Gregg mused out loud.

His partner bent down over the nearest dolphin.

"Look at the eyes," he said.

Ryan and Gregg joined him.

Blood.

This dolphin was starting to bleed from behind his eyelids.

"He'll never make it," Mitchell remarked. "I doubt if the poor creature's got more than a few minutes left, at most. Even if we manage to get it out into the water, well, it'll do no good."

Ryan rushed over to the other one.

No blood yet.

"Let's go, Ryan," Mitchell said. "We should be leaving here now."

"No!" Ryan shouted.

"But—," Mitchell protested.

"We've got to try! Don't you see, sir, *two of the dolphins out there saved my life!* But even if those two are gone somewhere else, I owe it to the rest of them!"

The two men glanced at one another.

"We were wondering how you got this distance away from the *S. S. Oceanic,"* Gregg admitted.

"Please, do this for me!" Ryan begged them both.

There was no hesitation after that. Working together, they managed to get one of the dolphins into water deep enough that it was able to float, after a fashion.

Even as the three humans stood with water up to their waists, several of the other dolphins swam over to their comrade and grouped themselves around it, guiding it out further into the ocean.

103

"Maybe that one will survive," Mitchell observed. "There was no blood in its eyes."

Just then they heard the sound of another helicopter approaching.

Twenty

The reunion between the Bartletts was so warm and joyous that Gregg and Mitchell looked at one another, realizing how much they missed their own families. They worked in the Caribbean area five days a week and then flew back home to Florida on weekends.

Andrew Bartlett and Chad started to turn back toward the helicopter that had brought them to that island.

"Wait!" Ryan said excitedly. "There's one more dolphin. There—."

Mitchell came up to him, put his hand on Ryan's shoulder.

"It's nearly gone, Ryan," he said. "There's no point—."

"There *is* a point," Ryan shot back. "It's awful to die alone like that."

"But that dolphin was probably out of it half an hour ago," Mitchell tried to make him understand.

"We don't *know* that!"

"What's going on, Ryan?" Mr. Bartlett interrupted.

"No time, Dad," his son said. "Trust me. I'll tell you later. Let's hurry . . . *please!*"

Trust me.

Coming from Ryan, that was good enough for Andrew Bartlett.

In less than a minute, they all, including the two wrestlers, had gathered around that last dolphin, by far the biggest of the three, in fact, nearly as large as a good-sized shark. Slowly they pushed it toward the water, inch by inch, until it was floating.

Several of the other dolphins swam over to their dying comrade, grouped themselves around it, and guided it out further into the ocean.

The same!

But, this time the group of them didn't leave immediately.

"They're still hanging around," Ryan observed. "What do they want?"

Chad's answer surprised him.

"Over there," he said, pointing to the spot back on shore. "The one that's dead."

"They want the body in the ocean!" Ryan said, catching his brother's meaning, and moving as quickly as he could back through the water. "They want it where it belongs."

The dead one was the youngest, it seemed, and the lightest. There was no trouble moving it into the water, but the body started to sink as soon as they let go.

So Ryan and Chad grabbed it and held on.

Something astonishing happened then.

Four of the dolphins approached within inches of Ryan and Chad. One of the creatures stuck its snout up through the water and started making a chattering sound, opening and closing its mouth in a particularly excited manner.

"Shove him forward, Ryan," Chad said.

Ryan nodded, and the two of them pushed the lifeless body ahead of them.

As soon as it started to disappear below the surface, those four dolphins swam over to it, and, between them, nudged it back to the surface.

"They don't know yet that it's gone," Ryan said, his voice husky with emotion. "They—."

But the dolphins caught on quickly enough.

"Look!" Chad shouted.

Everyone *did* look. Everyone saw the four mammals begin a mournful chorus of sorts, which lasted for a minute or so. Then the dolphins guided the body of their comrade between them as they swam out in the ocean. When they rejoined the others, the whole group took up that sad, sad chorus.

"Maybe one of the others made it," Chad said hopefully. "Maybe this was the only dolphin that died."

"Could be," Ryan said. "But at least we did what we could."

Chad waded over to him, and they embraced, having no reason to feel ashamed that the group waiting on shore saw them crying.

Epilogue

Andrew Bartlett arranged for the rest of their so-called vacation to be spent in Hawaii, on the island of Oahu. The agency for which he worked, with the full cooperation of the U. S. State Department, maintained several homes there for exactly that purpose: rest and recreation for their agents. All of the houses were located in the central portion of Oahu, in areas that seemed untouched by the business interests of the rest of the island.

At first, Ryan thought it was just a coincidence, what with Cindy Farnsworth and Sea Life Park being there and this happening just after their ordeal at sea.

But then he realized that his father must have set it up on purpose, because coincidences like that just didn't happen!

The morning after they arrived, Ryan found out how correct he was when Mr. Bartlett asked if

Ryan wanted to go to Sea Life Park after breakfast.

The three of them were sitting out on the lawn in bamboo-framed wicker chairs around a round table. Flowers filled the air with a dozen different scents. In front of each of them, on oversized plates, were slices of pineapple, guavas, papaya, along with ample helpings of scrambled eggs, whole-wheat toast and special Hawaiian jellies. Their guest house had come with one of the best cooks in all the islands.

"I thought so!" Ryan exclaimed.

"Maybe Cindy's not working today," Chad added, hating the idea that she might not be.

"She is," their father said simply, and he noticed that his two sons were staring in amazement.

Experiencing the approach to Sea Life Park was always half the fun for first-timers, especially since few of them could ever be truly prepared for the stunning sight that awaits them.

That was an especially thrilling moment in each case . . . when they swung their cars around the turn directly up to the park and saw the turquoise water on one side and the lush, green-covered mountains on the other, with the park squarely in the middle. Many pulled over to the black-dirt shoulder and just sat there, looking at the beauty

110

of that spot, inhaling the clean air, listening to the calls of brightly-colored birds.

Andrew Bartlett and his sons had made that ride along the coast a dozen times over the years, never, never tiring of it. They were always able to count on it to cheer them up, to take their minds away from smog-filled air, noisy, clogged freeways, and threats of bombs and whatever else.

Chad couldn't wait to hop out of the car when they parked, but he stopped suddenly, and turned back toward the car.

"What's wrong?" Ryan asked as he was getting out.

"I think Cindy's great," Chad told him, "and maybe we can spend a little time together later, but right now it's important for you to be with her alone."

Ryan knew that Chad was not some sort of cold-hearted fiend, but this kind of sensitivity took him by surprise

"Is that fair, Chad?" he asked. "She likes us both."

"The Lord used those dolphins to save your life, Ryan. You need to return a little of what they did, in some way to learn more about them from Cindy."

Chad smiled, then: "Hey, I'm just a dumb jock. What do I know about stuff like that?"

Mr. Bartlett put his arms around both sons.

"Chad and I will be fine," he said. "Do what you have to, son. We'll be here if you need us."

Ryan smiled, thanked the two of them, then headed off toward the exhibit.

"I've never known creatures like them," Cindy Farnsworth was saying. "Dogs can get mean—just look at those pit bulls, if you need proof of that. Cats really dig into you with their claws or their teeth or both if you rub them the wrong way. Parrots are a problem sometimes, too. But—."

She waved her hand in the direction of the three dolphins in the aquarium.

"But those beautiful, beautiful mammals—you have no idea how consistent they are. You can use them, and abuse them, but they never *ever* turn on you."

"Why?" Ryan asked. "I can study them all I want, but I just don't *live* with these wonderful creatures the way you do. Why them? Do you have any idea, Cindy? Do you have some clues, even?"

He thought back to a moment he had shared with his father.

"Dad says some people today put animals on a pedestal," Ryan continued. "They seem to be worshiping the creature instead of the Creator."

"Yeah," Cindy agreed, "that's a problem. But we don't ignore abuses because some crazy folks have taken up the cause. There are false prophets, hypocrites in the Church right now, but that doesn't mean we turn our backs on *all* ministries."

She was making a lot of sense.

"You love dolphins, don't you?" he asked her.

"I do, Ryan, a lot. They save lives; they bring joy to people who attend this park. Everything they do is good."

"Some people tell me that it seems far-fetched," said Ryan, "to think that dolphins know what's going on when they happen to do what they did with me . . . that it's just chance or luck or whatever."

"No *way!*" Cindy said. "I'll prove it to you."

"Yeah?" Ryan replied, excited. "How?"

"Just watch!"

She climbed up the metal steps a few feet away, and *fell* into the water, and started screaming.

In an instant all three dolphins swam to her side and gathered around her, chattering with obvious great concern. She reached out and hugged each one, then climbed onto a platform built into the side of the aquarium. Only then, apparently after seeing that she didn't seem to be hurt, did they return to the game that they had been playing among themselves.

"Once a little girl stumbled and fell into the tank," Cindy said after drying herself off a bit. "Not more than three seconds later, one of them had gotten under her and nudged her back to the surface. Every few months, something like that will happen that proves, as far as I am concerned, that God has something pretty special in mind for creatures like them."

She realized that she had started crying, overcome by memories. Ryan took a tissue out of a side pocket in his jeans, and handed it to her.

"What a gentleman you are!" she said.

She waved her hand through the air as though to clear it of the bittersweet memories.

"Enough!" she said. "My shift is over about now. Why don't we all get together for dinner? It's my treat."

"But Dad wouldn't allow that," Ryan protested.

"You mean from a girl?"

"Well, yeah. Something like that."

"Tell your Dad that he's never met a *woman* like this one!" she said, smiling from ear to ear.

As they left the enclosure, Ryan could hear the three dolphins joining together in a kind of chorus.

His eyes widened.

"Are they—?" he started to ask.

"—saying good-bye?"

Ryan stammered, at a loss for words.

Cindy reached out and took his hand.

"What do *you* think?" she asked as they went to look for Mr. Bartlett and Chad.

Ryan had a pretty good idea what the answer was.

DON'T MISS THESE OTHER BARTLETT BROTHER ADVENTURES:

Sudden Fear
When Ryan Bartlett accidently intercepts a computer message, he and his brother are stalked by terrorists who plan to destroy a nuclear power plant. (ISBN 0–8499–3301–3)

The Frankenstein Project
While visiting a friend in the hospital, Ryan and Chad Bartlett come face to face with mysterious children and secret scientific experiments. (ISBN 0–8499–3303–X, available in September 1991)

Forbidden River
The brothers find themselves in the midst of an international conflict when their father, who is a U. S. diplomat, is kidnapped by drug lords in South America. (ISBN 0–8499–3304–8, available in September 1991)

ABOUT THE AUTHOR:

Award-winning author Roger Elwood is well known for his suspense-filled stories for both youth and adult readers. His twenty-six years of editing and writing experience include stories in *Today's Youth* and *Teen Life* magazines and a number of best-selling novels for Scholastic Book Clubs and Weekly Reader Book Clubs. He has also had titles featured by Junior Literary Guild and Science Fiction Book Club. Among his most outstanding adult books is *Angel Walk*, a winner of the Angel Award from Religion in Media.